Dana Winthers
1971

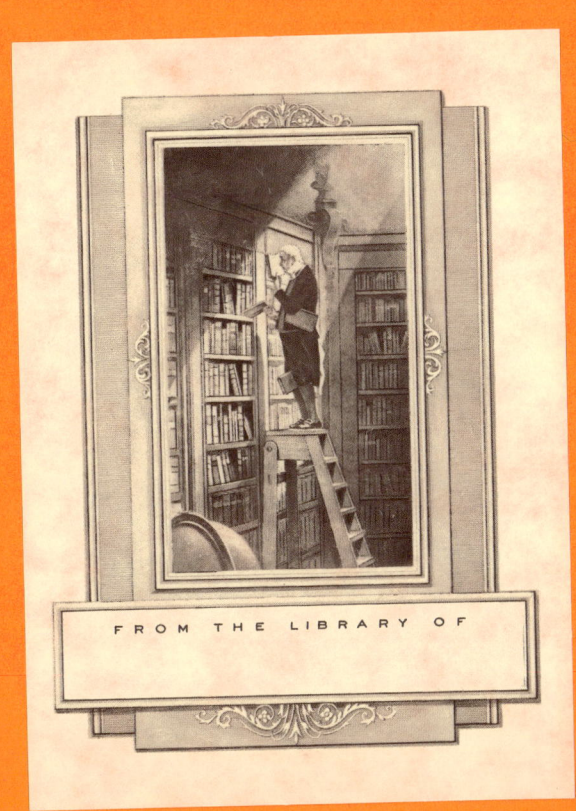

FROM THE LIBRARY OF

SEP 10 1979

PR
2892
S94

We Are Such Stuff As Dreams Are Made On

[*The Tempest,* IV/i]

Dick Corten: *Page* 25. Bill Eppridge, *Life* Magazine, ® Time Inc.: *Page* 9. Bonnie Freer: *Pages* 17, 23. Carter Hamilton: *Pages* 3, 11, 12, 13, 15, 19, 20, 30. Mike Mauney, *Life* Magazine, ® Time Inc.: *Page* 5. Fred W. McDarrah: *Pages* 4, 18, 21, 27, 29. Mickey Pfleger: *Pages* 16, 26. Arthur Tress: *Page* 7. United Press International Photos: *Page* 24. Burk Uzzle, Magnum: *Page* 8.

Copyright ® 1971 by Hallmark Cards, Inc., Kansas City, Missouri. All Rights Reserved.
Printed in the United States of America. Library of Congress Catalog Card Number: 74-155447; Standard Book Number: 87529-225-9.

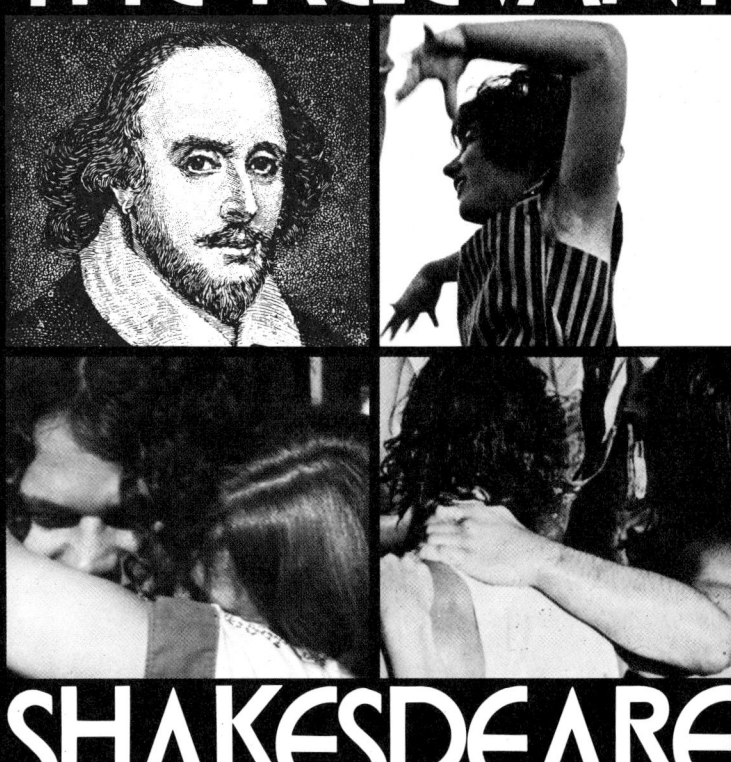

WE ARE SUCH STUFF AS DREAMS ARE MADE ON...

[*The Tempest*, IV/i]

Selected by
Roland I. Swanson, Jr.

SHAKESPEARE ON YOUTH

These trees shall be my books.
[*As You Like It*, III/ii]

I would be friends with you,
and have your love.
[*The Merchant of Venice*, I/iii]

Under the greenwood tree
Who loves to lie with me…
 [*As You Like It*, II/v]

The idea of her life shall sweetly creep
Into his study of imagination,
And every lovely organ of her life
Shall come apparell'd in more precious habit,
More moving-delicate, and full of life
Into the eye and prospect of his soul.
                [*Much Ado About Nothing*, IV/i]

We still have slept together,
Rose at an instant, learn'd, play'd,
    eat together;
And whereso'er we went, like Juno's swans,
Still we went coupled and inseparable.
                    [*As You Like It*, I/iii]

And bleat the one at the other; what we chang'd
Was innocence for innocence; we knew not
The doctrine of ill-doing, nor dream'd
We were as twinn'd lambs that did
    frisk i' the sun
That any did.

[*The Winter's Tale*, I/ii]

Now my soul hath elbow-room.
[*King John*, V/vii]

If music be the food of love, play on…

[*Twelfth Night*, I/i]

Love comforteth like sunshine after rain.

[*Venus and Adonis*]

Now join your hands, and with your hands
your hearts.

[*Henry VI*, Pt. III, IV/vi]

We few,
we happy few,
we band
of brothers.
[*Henry V*, IV/iii]

What's mine is yours, and what is yours is mine.
[*Measure for Measure*, V/i]

Shall I compare thee to a summer's day?
Thou art more lovely and more temperate…
[*SONNET 18*]

O spirit of love! how quick and fresh art thou…

[*Twelfth-Night*, I/i]

Even now I tremble to think your father, by some accident,
Should pass this way, as you did: O, the Fates!
…What would he say? Or how should I…behold
The sternness of his presence?

[*The Winter's Tale,* IV/iv]

Our remedies oft in ourselves do lie…
[*All's Well That Ends Well*, I/i]

True, I talk of dreams…
   [*Romeo and Juliet,* I/iv]

I never heard a passion so confus'd,
So strange, outrageous, and so variable...

[*Merchant of Venice*, II/viii]

But in the gross
and scope
of my opinion,
This bodes some
strange eruption
to our state.
[*Hamlet*, I/i]

Speak what we feel, not what we ought to say.

[*King Lear*, V/iii]

Still in thy right hand carry gentle peace,
To silence envious tongues: be just, and fear not.

[*Henry VIII*, III/ii]

As many arrows, loosed several ways,
Fly to one mark;
So may a thousand actions, once a foot,
End in one purpose,
And be all well borne
Without defeat.

[*Henry V*, I/ii]